How to Edit Cookery Books

Recipes, ingredients, measurements and methods

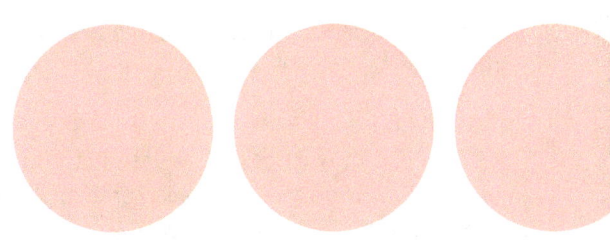

Wendy Hobson

First published in the UK in 2021 by
Chartered Institute of Editing and Proofreading
Apsley House
176 Upper Richmond Road
London
SW15 2SH

ciep.uk

Copyright © 2021 Chartered Institute of Editing and Proofreading

ISBN 978 1 915141 04 0 (print)
ISBN 978 1 915141 05 7 (PDF ebook)

All rights reserved. No part of this publication may be reproduced or used in any manner without written permission from the publisher, except for quoting brief passages in a review.

The moral rights of the author have been asserted.

The information in this work is accurate and current at the time of publication to the best of the author's and publisher's knowledge, but it has been written as a short summary or introduction only. Readers are advised to take further steps to ensure the correctness, sufficiency or completeness of this information for their own purposes.

Development editing, copyediting and proofreading by CIEP members Liz Dalby, Cathy Tingle, Margaret Hunter, Myriam Birch, Michelle Bullock.

Typeset in-house
Original design by Ave Design (**avedesignstudio.com**)
Image credits: 2, Shutterstock/Tania Zbrodko; 21, Pixabay/Kai Reschke; 30, Pixabay/Jenny Porter; 49, Pixabay/Manfred Richter; 70, Pixabay/Kawita Chitprathak.

Contents

1 |	Introduction	1
	My experience	1
	Who is this guide for?	3
2 |	Getting started	5
	The brief	5
	General text issues to look out for	10
3 |	The role of the cookery copyeditor	11
	How do you know the recipes will work?	12
	When should you check with the author?	13
4 |	Editing the supporting text	14
	The concept	14
	The author	15
	Equipment, techniques and ingredients	15
	Notes on the recipes	16
	Some differences for blogs or web copy	17
5 |	Editing the recipes	18
	Recipe titles	19
	Recipe introductions	20
	Number of servings	20
	Additional recipe information	22
	The photographs	23

6	The ingredients	24
	Order of ingredients	24
	Descriptions	24
	Measurements	30
	Subdividing ingredients	33
	Serving suggestions	35
	International measures	35
7	Preparation of ingredients	36
	Quantity and description	36
	Applying common sense	38
	Complex preparation	39
8	The method	40
	Ordering the text	40
	Equipment	43
	Preparation in advance	44
	Ingredient specifics	47
	Techniques	48
	Timings and results	49
	Subdividing the method	51
9	Recipes for international markets	52
	Spellings and names	52
	Conversions	54
	Cooking with cups	55
	Keeping it simple	57
10	International conversions and alternatives	60
	British (US) English cooking terms	60
	Basic liquid conversions	62
	Basic weight conversions	63
	Basic cup conversions	64
	Oven temperature conversions	65
	Linear measurement conversions and pan sizes	65

11 | Additional notes 66
    Fonts and symbols 66
    Automating tasks on cookery manuscripts 67

12 | Proofreading recipes 68

13 | Applying cookery editing skills to other texts 69

1 | Introduction

This guide is an introduction to copyediting recipes and cookery texts. The aim is to provide an understanding of how recipes work, and the logical and practical thinking that needs to be applied when editing texts for publication.

My experience

This guide draws on my four decades of experience as an author, commissioning editor, recipe tester and copyeditor, beginning at a time when cookery publishing was a shadow of its current self. The development of this area of the market, and its spread from print to online, has been phenomenal. A glance at how much things have changed, and continue to develop, demonstrates both the opportunities for copyeditors and the reasons why there are so many decisions for them to make.

In the 1970s, most cookery books only included one set of imperial measurements, so there was no need for conversions. The style of cooking was akin to what our mothers passed down (and I use the gender-specific word advisedly), and even the most notable market success, the *Hamlyn All Colour Cook Book* – published, not uncommonly, without a cover byline for one Mary Berry – was still offering 'Bacon Jacket Potatoes' and 'Marble Cake'. For the ordinary cook, ingredients for international dishes were hard to come by, so the books had to contain explanations of new and unfamiliar ingredients, along with suitable alternatives for those who hunted high and low to find them (sun-dried tomatoes? tofu? ajwain?) to no avail. There were few well-known TV chefs, the term 'celebrity chef' had yet to be coined and, of course, we had no key to the world of discovery that is the internet.

The rules were therefore basic; we had to evolve them. And as our knowledge grew, as colour printing was introduced more widely and as the market expanded, we had to change those rules to keep pace so that the presentation of information in the books continued to reflect the needs of the home cook.

It would be impossible for every editor to be an expert in every topic they undertake; it is not our job to be the expert, and I am not an expert chef. However, some familiarity with and proficiency in the subject are always helpful, beyond basic training and experience in copyediting. In this case, that means some knowledge of cookery, of course, and also a practical mindset.

This guide is therefore the result of many years of honing editorial techniques on all kinds of cookery texts, from the works of top cooks and chefs – including Mary Berry, Gary Rhodes and Ken Hom – to experienced professional food writers and home cooks who want to share their culinary creations.

1 | Introduction

Who is this guide for?

The guide is primarily designed for copyeditors and is addressed to them, but will also prove useful for anyone involved with cookery texts:

- publishers
- commissioning editors
- desk editors
- cookery authors
- proofreaders
- indexers
- recipe developers and testers
- bloggers
- website writers and editors
- magazine editors and contributors
- newspaper staff
- marketing staff for food retailers
- photographers
- stylists
- home economists.

All these professionals need to know – to a greater or lesser extent – how to write, present and accurately interpret recipes.

> ### Editing practical books
> Although this guide focuses on food, you can also learn from it about editing any kind of practical text by extrapolating from food to anything from woodworking to painting (see **Applying cookery editing skills to other texts**).

The main focus of the guide is the process of editing the recipes themselves, but it also offers advice on how general editing tasks and principles sometimes need to be subtly adjusted for cookery texts.

Any book or written work can benefit from professional editorial attention, and cookery writing requires a good editor just as much as any academic or fiction work. This guide will help anyone tasked with working on a cookery text to ensure that it is produced to the highest standards and delivers great eating.

2 | Getting started

Before you start work on the detail of editing recipes, it is important to look at the broader context of the project on which you are working. You need to have a clear idea of your responsibilities and where you fit in the team.

The creative team in the editorial process for a cookery text will vary depending on the circumstances; a publisher will be different from a self-publishing author or a blogger creating recipes for their website. Clearly no single project will involve all the people this guide is designed for and projects will be organised in different ways, but you need to know precisely what is expected and how you relate to other professionals so there is no danger of a job falling between you and another member of the team. Whoever is commissioning the editing work, I have referred to them in this guide as the client.

The brief

Your principal responsibility is bringing the text up to the standard expected for publication. Specifically in cookery, your objective is to achieve the best outcome for the reader: they should be able to obtain the ingredients and follow the instructions in order to cook an enjoyable meal. As the copyeditor, this involves answering a series of questions to which the answers are not always yes or no; they frequently involve an if or a but. To be equipped to find the answers for your particular project, you will need some background information, which should be provided in a comprehensive brief that explains the nature of the job, the status of the text supplied and the details of what you are expected to do.

Much of the briefing will happen via email, but don't forget that sometimes a phone call or a video chat can help you establish a good working relationship and resolve queries much more quickly and effectively.

A client experienced in the publishing process will follow a system and know what you need; for other clients, it is up to you to make suggestions or ask questions until the project details are clear.

You will obviously need the basic text to work on, but the more you can find out about the project, such as the background information in the following list, the better your position to make the right editorial decisions.

- **Text:** You should be supplied with a complete text document, and you will often have a page plan, which should match the manuscript (if not, you may need to reorder the recipes). Sometimes authors produce each recipe in a single document, in which case you'll need the running order so you can create a workable manuscript.
- **Author details:** The author's credentials and contact details, if you will be sending your queries direct (rather than through the client).
- **Level of edit:** An expectation of the level of edit is useful, for example if the text will need particularly heavy editing.
- **Design and production details:** The book specification, number of recipes and any length constraints. If a design is available, it can be useful to see a presentation spread or, for an established cookery publisher, another book in the same series or by the same author.
- **Market definition:** Territories in which the book is being sold, which will affect the measurements and terminology you include.
- **Style guide:** If your client has a house style, this will be the basis for your project style sheet. As well as all the usual style choices, you will need to include:
  » conversion tables
  » how conversions and international terminology are displayed
  » whether or not you specify peeling carrots and onions, for example
  » use of terms such as 'can' or 'tin'
  » whether methods are in paragraphs or numbered points
  » capitalisation of headings and subheadings.

- **Concept and background:** Any set of recipes with an unusual concept and unique selling proposition needs that USP to be applied throughout the organisation, presentation, content and detail of the recipes themselves. For example, a less familiar international cuisine may need extra guidance on ingredients or techniques; special-diet books will contain nutritional information.
- **Readership:** The level of detail required in instructions varies depending on whether the reader is new to cooking or is an experienced cook. Think how frustrating it is for an expert to be told the difference between folding and whisking – and how equally important it is to explain that difference to a novice.
- **Additional tasks:** Establish if you are expected to write caption copy, prepare or check the page plan, check the layouts or other jobs. Ask whether your feedback would be appreciated on the quality of the recipes or their structure and organisation. Your fresh pair of eyes is ideally positioned to spot an important recipe that has been missed out, or one that is clearly in the wrong place – an apple crumble in the brunches, or a beef casserole in the vegetarian section.
- **Photographs:** Define whether or not you are checking that the photographs match the recipes. It is unusual for a copyeditor to be asked to deal with resolution, output format, permissions or other technical aspects.
- **Markup:** Clarify any instructions on how you should mark up the text for layout, such as formatting fractions and indicating heading styles, including whether the text should be tagged.
- **Schedule:** Be realistic about the schedule dates. Remember to allow for author input and check their other commitments; they may be on the photoshoot just when you want them to be answering queries. If a delay is unavoidable, inform the team as soon as you become aware so they can adapt their schedules accordingly. Explain the reason and try to offer a solution at the same time as acknowledging a problem.
- **Fee for the job:** Ensure that the fee is appropriate for the scope of the work.

Working in batches

If not all the text is available, check whether there is time to wait for a complete manuscript before you start; try to avoid working in batches as it means more cross-checking. In any event, double-check that any additional copy or last-minute changes will come to you in a Word document with Track Changes or clearly listed and referenced to the text so that you can take them in to your main manuscript. It is not unusual to receive a revised manuscript document from an author with, say, 20 random changes in a 100-recipe document, giving you the extra work of comparing them to find those alterations. Even though this is now an automated process, it takes time and introduces margin for error.

Assessing the work

Look at the text and the brief carefully and make sure you have everything you need. You might find that a skim through the text will raise questions on style or content that you can clarify with the client and resolve before you start work, avoiding the need for lengthy query lists at a later stage:

- Note anything missing from the text that was supposed to be included, such as separate cooking times or special-diet icons. If this affects the whole text, it is better to resolve it early on than have individual queries on every recipe.
- If the author has used styles that don't conform to the style sheet, confirm whether you should retain the author's style – for example 'salt and freshly milled black pepper' instead of 'sea salt and freshly ground black pepper'.
- If you are deciding on points of style for the project (rather than following an established house style), make sure the client is happy with your conversions and presentation.

A good way to tackle this is to edit a couple of recipes to confirm that your approach and decision-making is accepted by the client, especially if you are developing your own conversions. This is also good to give you a feel for the amount of work involved.

This is especially useful if a book is a compilation or has multiple authors, or if the author is working with a recipe developer. In those instances, you are likely to find a wide variety of styles that need to be made consistent and it is advisable to check that everyone involved is happy with the decisions you are making.

Editing your own recipes

If you are copyediting your own recipes, perhaps for a book or a blog, try to separate the roles of author and copyeditor. Complete all the work you would assign to the author, then take a break, if you can, and come back to the text as copyeditor; your focus will be slightly different and you will be able to look at the text more objectively.

This is because when you read something familiar, your brain tries to work more efficiently and extracts the most relevant information, projecting and making assumptions, so you read what you expect to find, especially if you read quickly. Not only does that mean you can easily miss typos, you can also skim over descriptions that could be confusing or open to misinterpretation.

✗ Stand in a pan of boiling water for 5 minutes.

✗ Bring to the boil and cover the pan. Add the onions and stir well.

For the same reason, it is best to employ a separate proofreader, but if that is not possible make sure you allow some time between the tasks.

General text issues to look out for

The quality of the text you receive can vary enormously. The author may present a clean and clear manuscript that adheres to consistent style, formatting and conversion rules – or they may not. A self-publishing author is perhaps less likely than a publisher to be aware of typical publishing conventions. Remember that the author is concentrating on the food and its flavours; you need to focus on polishing the delivery of that information, so that the reader can understand the recipe and replicate the dish.

Here are some issues you might encounter in a cookery author's text:

- An inexperienced author has not been adequately briefed or supervised by the commissioning editor.
- The author is used to restaurant quantities and has cut back the recipes inaccurately.
- The author has not followed the brief or has not been given one.
- The author usually cooks in handfuls, dashes and packets.
- It doesn't occur to the author that a packet can be different sizes because they are so used to using the same items.
- The author is so familiar with their subject area that they assume too much knowledge in the reader.
- The author assumes that everyone can obtain hard-to-find ingredients.
- The author is unfamiliar with publishing conventions, such as listing ingredients in order of use.

It is up to you to resolve these issues.

3 | The role of the cookery copyeditor

Your job as the copyeditor of cookery texts is essentially the same as any other non-fiction editor: to make sure the text is clear, elegant and informative, and fulfils its practical purpose. In this instance, that involves making sure the recipes:

- are accurate, easy to follow and unambiguous
- achieve the promised results
- make the reader feel comfortable with the consistency and reliability of the information.

There is also a creative element in that you should be questioning anything that doesn't fit the brief or that you expect will not turn out well. Ultimately, changing or dropping a recipe is not your decision but it is important that you raise any concerns as the client is unlikely to be as familiar with the details as you are. There is a simple way to help you achieve that.

Approaching the work
Try to read the recipes as though you are cooking them. Forget the desk, think worktop; forget the word processor, think food processor.

The best-practice mindset is to work step by step – mentally roll up your sleeves and put your apron on. Think about what the end user needs to know and make sure you tell them.

> ### Establish trust
> The reader will be made to feel confident by the accuracy and consistency of the text, and will be able to cook and enjoy the recipes as they were meant to be.

How do you know the recipes will work?

Since you are not actually testing the recipes, it will be impossible to say categorically that they work. However, by using your own practical experience and common sense, you will develop a good feeling for when a recipe might present difficulties.

Here are some danger signs to look out for:

- Cooking is started in an ordinary saucepan that is then transferred to the oven.
- A very high heat is recommended but with few ingredients.
- Ingredients are missing from the ingredients list or the method.
- A quantity is surprisingly large or small.
- A high oven temperature is combined with a long cooking time.
- A low temperature is combined with a very short cooking time.
- There are no instructions on what to expect at the end of a stage of cooking.
- A timing does not seem logical.
- Ingredients are out of sequence (although be warned that authors don't always put ingredients in order, so this may be something you have to correct on all recipes).
- The combination of ingredients is particularly unusual and no mention is made of that in the introduction.
- A conversion is suspect, with the imperial measurement wrong in relation to the metric equivalent.

When should you check with the author?

To allow the author and client to see your edits, if they wish, most editors work in Track Changes and use Word Comments to highlight queries. Establish at the outset how much intervention is expected so everyone is comfortable with the process.

There are many things that you should be able to resolve yourself rather than having to refer to the author:

- **There might be a simple typing error:** Don't bother the author asking if that 20°C should have been 200°C if it is obvious.
- **An ingredient may simply have been forgotten:** If it is clear that you add the garlic with the onions, just add it to the method. If something is in the method but not listed in the ingredients, add it with its quantity, checking that with the author if necessary.
- **Information is scant:** If a utensil or technique needs a clearer description, or a little more detail on timing or results, you may be able to follow the author's style and fill in the missing information.

However, if there is clearly a mistake or something you cannot resolve – something is missing or you don't understand an instruction; you find a savoury ingredient in your apple crumble or no method for making the ice cream – obviously you need to raise a query.

Make sure your questions are unambiguous, and when you suggest changes be sensitive to the fact that this is the author's work. Briefly explain your reasoning and the benefits of the changes, if they are not immediately obvious. Putting yourself in the place of the reader trying to cook the recipe for the first time is often a good way of helping an author be objective about the need for clarity on a technique that is second nature to them.

The author wants their recipes to be well received – so when you have finished working on their text, they should look at what you have done and see their work, with improvements. They should be happy that you have added value but not changed the essence.

4 | Editing the supporting text

The recipes themselves are rarely delivered without context, so although the amount and content of text in support of the recipes will vary considerably between books, websites, features or articles, there is likely to be additional background or practical information provided for you to edit. This may include:

- the concept and development of the recipes
- the author's background, experience and qualifications for writing the text
- essential equipment
- special techniques
- unusual ingredients.

You will need to make sure that this general text is appropriate for the project and provides everything the reader needs to know.

The concept

The book's inception, concept and intention or objective are all important to the reader, especially the level at which the recipes are pitched and therefore the expectation of the cook's expertise. The reader also wants to know how the recipes are organised, how to get the best out of the recipes, who the collection is designed for and any special features. Space might be given to a particular cooking style, seasonal foods or an international cuisine. Especially in books related to special diets or healthy eating, the text may include menu plans, calorie counters or nutritional information.

The author

In cookery texts, the status of the author is important both in terms of their credentials for putting any recipe collection together and in making sure their style and personality are properly reflected. With authors who are not used to writing in English, that may mean a sensitive approach to ensuring the language is correct and informative without compromising their unique voice.

Equipment, techniques and ingredients

Most cookbooks are designed to be used in home kitchens, with basic equipment available. An occasional piece of unusual equipment can be dealt with in the recipe text. However, if the recipes require several unfamiliar or specialist pieces of equipment, they are usually included in a separate section; for example, in a book of recipes for use with a breadmaker or other kitchen gadget.

Some cookery books, especially those for children or beginners, will need more detailed guidance on appropriate techniques or special skills, possibly with step-by-step instructions in addition to the recipes. A section on safety in the kitchen is often included in a children's book.

For the most part, ingredients should be available in major supermarkets. Individual recipes can provide alternatives if something is not so easy to obtain, but if there are a lot of unusual ingredients, a glossary section describing flavours, textures, availability, usage and possible alternatives is useful.

Magazines

All this contextualisation applies to magazines or features as much as to book publishing. Although with magazines and features you may be working to a much tighter word count and format, with a limited number of recipes, you will still need to establish a comfort zone for the reader by taking the above points into consideration within a more succinct text.

For the same reason, a book might include a list of suppliers or sources of ingredients or equipment. Bear in mind, though, that this kind of information dates easily and may need to be relevant to an international market. For online recipes, links can be more easily updated.

Notes on the recipes

Many books include a list of general notes on the principles followed in the recipes to avoid having to repeat them throughout the book. This can broaden the scope of the book to those readers who need a little more help, but it is not suitable for all books and its inclusion does not necessarily mean that you can omit information from the recipe pages. A lot of people don't actually read the general introductions!

Notes on the recipes could include things like:

- Wash all fresh ingredients before preparation.
- Cooking times are approximate.
- Adjust oven temperatures to suit your own oven as they are all slightly different.
- The recipes were tested in a fan oven at the temperatures given. For non-fan ovens, increase the oven temperature by 10–20°C.
- Eggs are medium unless listed otherwise.
- Recipes serve 4 unless indicated.
- Portion sizes are given on individual recipes.
- Spoon and cup measurements are level.
- 1 tsp = 5ml, 1 tbsp = 15ml; it is best to use culinary measuring spoons.
- The recipes specify unsalted butter but you can use any suitable butter or spread.
- Seasoning is a matter of personal taste.
- Always use fresh herbs unless dried are specified.
- Can sizes are approximate as they vary by brand.
- Don't mix metric, imperial and US measures; follow one set only.

Some differences for blogs or web copy

By definition, a recipe blog or web copy works in a different way from recipe text in print and demands special writing and editing skills that can be acquired through training and experience. Here are a few of the primary differences that make recipes intended for digital platforms different from print:

- Background information tends to be presented as a lead-in to the recipes or even as separate, linked pages.
- Regular recipe blogs focus on an individual recipe with a longer, more chatty introduction in a colloquial style.
- There are plenty of subheadings and the copy tends to be broken up into blocks.
- It is easy to create links to additional information, asides or alternatives from the main text; make sure there is always an easy way back to the main recipe.
- The text is specifically written to include relevant keywords for search engine optimisation (SEO).
- Digressions on ingredients can be slotted into the text.
- The copy is often linked direct to other recipes, websites or suppliers.
- Text is usually interspersed with photographs of the recipe under construction.
- The recipe text itself is most usually given in one set of measurements.
- Converted versions of the recipes are often supplied separately, so that you can click to view the recipe in metric or US measures rather than having them all on one recipe.
- The audience is always global.
- Options can also be provided to allow a change in the number of servings resulting in a recalculation of the quantities.
- Text and recipes can be updated or amended after the initial publication.

5 | Editing the recipes

When it comes to editing the individual recipes, your aim should be to make them coherent and unambiguous. All recipes will include:

- a title
- introductory notes
- the number of servings
- the ingredients
- the method.

Some recipes may include:

- serving suggestions
- hints and tips
- alternative ingredients
- single or separate cooking and preparation times
- nutritional information
- allergen information
- estimated ingredient costs
- storage times and instructions
- notes on refrigerating and freezing.

The copyeditor needs to check that each element relevant to the project is included accurately and consistently across all recipes.

Recipe titles

Titles might be informative or frivolous, depending on the text or author voice, but be consistent; a jaunty title such as 'Mike's Favourite Weekend Breakfast' may look out of place amid descriptive titles like 'Crushed Avocado on Sourdough with Sweet Chutney'.

Make sure the title reflects the recipe and does not mention an ingredient that is not in the dish. This sounds obvious, but authors often adapt and develop recipes during the testing phase and can easily forget to change an ingredient in the title when they have substituted something during testing that was more readily available or that worked better.

Avoid multi-language mix-ups like 'Swordfish in Sauce Pomodoro' or 'Chicken à la Béarnaise'.

Books on international cuisine may have an English and an original-language title. Make sure you have both for all the recipes and that they are consistently in the same order; usually the original title is first in a restaurant-style book for experienced cooks but the English is first in more everyday books. When you include cross-references between recipes, use the primary title.

If you are able to check foreign-language titles that are to be printed in non-Latin alphabets, do so. If not, especially if the text is in a different script – such as Arabic or Thai – leave them well alone and make it clear that you have not checked them.

When you finalise the titles, think about how easily the readers will be able to find what they are looking for. Someone flicking through a book looking for a beef casserole, for example, may well pass by 'My Favourite Meat with Carrots'. This would also only be indexed if there is room for a comprehensive index that, as well as titles, lists recipes under each main ingredient. It won't be as well picked up by search engines.

Finally, be consistent in whether titles use sentence case or title case for all important words. Longer, descriptive titles tend to be more accessible in sentence case.

Recipe introductions

Most recipes start with a highly descriptive flavour snapshot of the dish, something like an extended restaurant menu description, often including personal anecdotes and comments. It is also a good place to mention special techniques or additional equipment, unique flavour combinations or sources, or alternatives for anything that is hard to come by.

There is no standard length for recipe introductions and they can vary from a sentence to full pages of text. They are likely to be of a similar length for each recipe within a book, although even this is not prescriptive so discuss it with the client if necessary.

Number of servings

Most recipes use a base of four servings; this is the default reader expectation. Servings are usually indicated at the top of the recipes as a serving number or a finished quantity.

> Serves 4
>
> Makes 300ml
>
> Makes 300ml to serve 4

Avoid vague and unhelpful statements.

> ✗ Makes a jar

You need to be specific.

> Makes 1 × 450g jar

5 | Editing the recipes

The four-serving default can be changed to any number, so a breakfast book is more likely to be for two, or a book on dinner parties or barbecues for six or ten. This variation might also happen between chapters: a book on recipes for the weekend might have breakfasts for two, brunches and lunches for four and an evening drinks party for eight. If so, this is usually highlighted in the chapter or general introduction, or in the **notes on the recipes**.

The reason for keeping all the recipes to the same serving quantity is not just an editorial nicety. Having cooked one or two recipes, the reader will instinctively relate the author's quantities to their own needs and will buy ingredients accordingly. That will not turn out well if they are making a recipe that they have assumed is for four when it is actually for eight – or worse, for two and they have invited guests.

When a recipe is highlighted as being adaptable for different numbers of people, the quantities should make it easy to factor up or down, so watch out for quantities such as one egg if the recipe says it can easily be halved.

Additional recipe information

Any of the following additional information might be included, in which case you should check that each point is accurately and consistently applied. Some might be presented as icons for instant recognition, others included as separate notes.

- **Cooking and preparation times:** Separate times for cooking and preparation, or one time for cooking and preparation together.
- **Difficulty level:** Specify this so that readers are not disappointed by what they perceive as too much or too little information.
- **Calories:** If calories are given, it is usually for one serving.
- **Nutritional information:** Quantities of fat and protein or other detailed nutritional information is often included in more specialist recipes or special-diet books and also specified per serving.
- **Shopping lists:** Sometimes divided into store cupboard and fresh ingredients, lists appear in some books and commonly in web-based recipes, linked to a food supplier.
- **Dietary or allergy information:** Whether the recipe is vegan, vegetarian, gluten-free, sugar-free or suitable for another specific dietary requirement is often indicated by an icon. Remember to check that the ingredients listed conform to the designation. You aren't going to miss biscuits in a gluten-free recipe or an egg in a vegan one, but it is easy to miss hidden ingredients – gluten in sausages, for example, or prohibited ingredients in a sauce or condiment: Worcestershire sauce contains anchovies; gelatine is found in some desserts. However, there are now so many 'free-from' varieties available, these can be specified in the ingredients.
- **Hints and tips:** Anything from alternative ingredients, shortcuts and variations to using leftovers is appropriate here. This spot is sometimes used for anecdotal information, although that is more often included in the introduction.
- **Alternatives and variations:** These are sometimes supplied separately.
- **Shortcuts:** If the shortcut is really useful, consider whether it should be in the method instead.
- **Using up leftovers:** This is especially useful if the serving quantities are large.

The photographs

Whether the photographs are supplied with the text or whether the photoshoot is planned for after the text has been edited, you should check at the outset whether it is your job to ensure that the photographs and recipes match. It is quite common for changes to be made – for visual effect, if ingredients are unavailable or if the author thinks of a last-minute improvement – especially to things like garnishes, dish shapes or accompaniments. For example, if the photo shows a dish garnished with rosemary and the text uses sage, then the text needs to be altered to use 'rosemary' or perhaps 'rosemary or sage'. A cake that is round in the photograph should not be cooked in a square tin in the text. If an ingredient or garnish has been inadvertently left out of a photograph, you can list it as optional.

Provide or check caption copy, if required. If the recipe and its accompanying photograph are displayed opposite each other across a spread, captions are not necessary. If they are needed, establish a consistent style. They probably only need the recipe title and page reference.

6 | The ingredients

When you come to the recipes themselves, start by tackling the ingredients. When you copyedit the ingredients, you should check that everything is included, clearly described and in sequence.

Order of ingredients

Always list the ingredients in the order in which they are used in the recipe.

There are two exceptions. Salt and pepper for seasoning are normally listed at the end unless a specific quantity is given. Additional ingredients for garnishing savoury dishes or decorating sweet dishes also appear at the end.

Descriptions

Although you will be editing to your style sheet, you will have established with your client how flexible that can be, such as being sensitive to author preference and using their chosen expressions instead of the client's usual style preferences.

> ### Language in cookery books
> While language in general text can be as imaginative as the author, in methods and ingredients lists, variety is the enemy! If you are used to other types of editing this may feel strange, but in cookery, it is preferable to use the same words and phrases each time for ingredients and for preparation and cooking techniques. This is all part of establishing trust and confidence for the reader so they know what is expected of them and that they will get good results.

Be consistent

Always use consistent descriptions rather than calling the same thing by different names. All the following are correct, but it is better to use one throughout the book.

> 5cm piece of root ginger
>
> thumb-sized ginger root
>
> 25g fresh root ginger

A reader will quickly get used to the mention of 'root ginger' and may trip up on 'ginger' on its own and wonder if they should use a different type, such as ground ginger, undermining their trust in the recipe.

Terms like 'small' should be avoided if possible: one person's small piece of ginger root might be someone else's idea of large.

Be consistent with spellings, taking particular note of anglicised words where it is common to see different variations.

> yogurt/yoghurt, pilau/pilaf, hummus/houmous

Non-English words that have not been anglicised are often put into italics, but this may vary in different books. In an Italian cookery book, you might decide that types of pasta are not to be in italics, whereas a quick and easy beginners' book might italicise more unusual varieties. Words that have been in use for so long that they have been absorbed into the language are not italicised.

> al fresco, al dente, *en chiffonade*

Include enough detail

Maintain an appropriate level of detail so the reader knows exactly which ingredient to use. Be careful with items that are available in different forms, especially when using the wrong type could spoil the recipe.

- **Flour:** Plain, self-raising, wholewheat, strong white, strong wholemeal, 00 flour, plus all the non-wheat flours.
- **Yeast:** Fresh, dried, instant.
- **Chocolate:** Milk, white, dark (with varying percentages of cocoa solids).
- **Ginger:** Root, shredded root, crystallised, ground.
- **Rice:** Long-grain, medium-grain, short-grain, pudding, basmati, easy-cook long-grain, risotto (and all the named types).

If an item is hard to come by, offer an alternative. If items are equally appropriate, list them separated by 'or'. If an item is a second choice, put the alternative in brackets. You can also use brackets to indicate that an ingredient is optional.

> 1 bunch of spring onions or 2 shallots, chopped
>
> 1 tbsp agave syrup (or raw sweetener)
>
> 1 tsp clear honey (optional)

Ingredients are uncooked by default, so specify if an ingredient, such as rice, is cooked. Both weight and characteristics will impact the recipe. It is usual to avoid brand names unless there is a particular reason for inclusion (unless, of course, the recipes are sponsored).

For cheeses, the word 'cheese' is usually omitted unless essential.

> Cheddar, Gouda, mozzarella, goat's cheese, cottage cheese

Prepositions

Prepositions are not usually used in the ingredients list.

> 50g raisins
>
> ✘ 50g of raisins

The exception is with expressions such as 'dash of', 'splash of', 'pinch of', 'drop of', 'zest of', 'handful of' or 'can of', which do take 'of' in most cookery texts. There are exceptions so follow the style and be consistent.

> 1 handful of raisins, 1 pinch of sea salt

Whether these expressions take a number, as here, or an 'a' is a matter of style, the former being the most common, but be consistent. Either of these options is correct, but don't mix them together.

> 1 splash of ..., grated zest of ½ lemon
>
> a splash of ..., grated zest of half a lemon

Abbreviations

The usual conventions for indicating measurements in ingredients lists are: mm, cm, g, kg, ml, litre, oz, lb, fl oz, tsp, tbsp, cup. Avoid variations and plurals, such as tbsps, which can be confusing. Litre is usually used in full as the letter l is easily confused with the figure 1. Don't use symbols such as " for inches as they are not recognised everywhere. A full point is not needed after units of measure.

In ingredients lists, use 'tsp' and 'tbsp' or 'teaspoons' and 'tablespoons' in full, according to style, but not a mixture. The abbreviations are more common. Use fl oz rather than pints, especially if the book has international potential (see the section on **Conversions**).

Capitalisation

Ingredients generally take lower case, even if they start a new line without a quantity, although house style may vary.

> juice of 1 lemon
>
> ✘ Juice of 1 lemon

Consistency is important in the use of upper case on ingredients. Produce takes an initial capital if it is named after a geographical region.

> Bordeaux, Champagne

This principle also applies to cheeses.

> Camembert, Cheddar, Roquefort
>
> goat's cheese, mozzarella

Proper nouns and branded goods (if used) should also be capitalised.

> Hungarian sausages, Tabasco sauce, Worcestershire sauce, Marmite

Seasoning, water and garnishing

Most books list the main seasoning ingredients as

>   sea salt and freshly ground black pepper

Some books might simply use 'seasoning', usually if they are for more experienced cooks.

Some publishers do not include water in the ingredients list, only the quantity in the method. However, if it is a measured quantity, it can be clearer for inexperienced cooks if it is treated as an ingredient and listed in sequence.

'Garnish' is used for savoury dishes and 'decorate' for sweet dishes. If the ingredient is specifically for the garnish or decoration, it is usually followed by a direction.

>   chopped parsley, to garnish
>
>   icing sugar, sifted, to decorate

If there are several garnish ingredients, it can be helpful if they are listed under a separate heading.

>   **For the garnish**
>
>   chopped parsley
>
>   lemon slices

Measurements

Recipes for the British English market usually include only metric measurements, although the client may choose to include imperial as well, if it is appropriate – perhaps the book is specifically for an older market, for example.

However, since many texts are published for a global market and must cater for the US, Australia and other regions, you may be expected to add conversion quantities for imperial and cup measures. See the section on **Recipes for international markets**.

Quantities

For some items, it is appropriate simply to use a number.

> 4 aubergines
>
> 3 carrots

6 | The ingredients

Small quantities are given in spoon measurements and it is best to use a proper set of measuring spoons for accuracy: 1 tsp = 5ml and 1 tbsp = 15ml. Spoon measurements are always level unless specified as 'heaped'. A dessert spoon is not a recognised measure (although it actually holds around 10ml).

Otherwise, specify the quantity in the same system in which the product is sold. Most are obvious but watch out for items like yogurt or condensed milk, which are sold in grams, whereas cream is sold in millilitres.

In ingredients lists, numerals are always used for numbers.

Spacing

The style sheet should indicate whether or not to include a space between the quantity and the measure; no space is more common (except for tsp and tbsp). If you are not sure, check with the client.

> 250g
>
> 250 g

A space is not needed between a number and a fraction (see also **Fonts and symbols**). Especially when fractions are unformatted, authors often include the space for clarity, but the figure will be clear once typeset.

> 11/2, 1½
>
> ✗ 1 ½, 1 1/2

Quantity ranges

If you need to include a quantity range, do not repeat the measure twice and do not elide quantity ranges. It is common practice to use a closed en rule, not a hyphen, between the figures.

100–125g unsalted butter

✘ 100g–125g unsalted butter

✘ 100-125g unsalted butter

✘ 120-40g unsalted butter

'About' is more commonly used than 'approximately' or 'approx.'. Whichever you use, there is no need to add a quantity or weight range at the same time.

100–125g fat-free yogurt

about 110g fat-free yogurt

✘ about 100–150g fat-free yogurt

✘ approx. 100–150g fat-free yogurt

Packets and cans

Always give the weight or size of packets and cans to avoid confusion. Use the weight of the can with its contents rather than the drained weight or contents weight (which you will find tucked away somewhere on the label).

400g can of chopped tomatoes

2 × 400g cans of chopped tomatoes

However, remember to check whether an author who specifies '400g chopped tomatoes' actually means a can of chopped tomatoes, chopped fresh tomatoes or one and a half cans of chopped tomatoes, which is the drained weight. They will all have an effect on the recipe.

Subdividing ingredients

Extremely long ingredients lists are off-putting and difficult to follow visually so they are better divided up to make the recipe easier to read.

Separate recipes

If part of the recipe can be made ahead, consider presenting that as a separate recipe with a cross-reference. This is particularly useful if a basic recipe is used several times within other recipes in the book. You may need to use one quantity of the referenced recipe or a specific amount. Decide whether recipe names are going to take lower case, sentence case or title case in cross-references and whether you are going to use 'of', then be consistent.

> 1 quantity of white sauce (see page xxx)
>
> 1 quantity of White sauce (see page xxx)
>
> 120ml White Sauce (see page xxx)

If you are using a specific quantity, make sure the original recipe indicates the full quantity so you can scale it up or down, or make a suggestion on how to use or store what is left over if you make but don't use the full quantity.

Dividing into elements

Another option if the ingredients list is unwieldy is to consider subdividing it into elements under subheadings. Without those headings, an entry might be:

> 100g Cheddar, half-sliced and half-grated

Split the relevant quantities under the subheadings, choosing descriptive titles for the subheadings to make them easier to identify and aid indexing and SEO.

> **For the cheese sauce**
>
> 50g Cheddar, sliced
>
> **For the cheese crumble topping**
>
> 50g Cheddar, grated

This also has an impact on the method (see **Subdividing the method**).

Reserving ingredients

Sometimes part of an ingredient is used, then the rest used later. In straightforward cases simply list the full quantity; using it will be dealt with in the section **Subdividing the method**.

If some of the ingredients are reserved for use later in the recipe or to provide a garnish or decoration, there are other choices. Let's say you are using 100g each of blueberries and chopped walnuts, with a few of each used for decoration. Having bought a 100g pack of blueberries, you would list the pack in the ingredients list, then, in the method, reserve a few before adding the bulk to the recipe. With a larger pack of walnuts, you could use the same technique, or you could specify using 100g in the recipe with a few more for decoration.

> 100g blueberries ... Reserve a few blueberries for decoration, then add the rest ...
>
> 100g walnuts, chopped ... Reserve a few walnuts for decoration, then add the rest ...
>
> 100g chopped walnuts, plus a few for decoration ... Add the walnuts ...

Serving suggestions

Sometimes suggestions for accompaniments or ways of serving the main dish are included at the end of the ingredients, sometimes not. They may be mentioned only in the ingredients, only after the method, only in the introduction or in any combination of these. Make the usage consistent.

If included in the ingredients list, serving suggestions appear at the end, either with a following note or under a subheading.

> steamed rice and vegetables of choice, to serve

> **To serve**
>
> steamed rice and vegetables of choice

International measures

The system of providing conversions for metric measurement, measuring with cups and other aspects of international recipe editing are covered in the section on **Recipes for international markets**.

7 | Preparation of ingredients

Ingredients in traditional cookery texts are intended to be gathered together and prepared before the reader starts to cook – imagine a kitchen like a TV studio where the cook has all the little bowls of prepared ingredients. Despite the fact that this does not represent most people's kitchens or methods of working, it is still the clearest way to present the ingredients. The importance of this to you as the copyeditor is that it helps you to ensure that the preparation of the ingredients is appropriate and consistent.

Move with the times

Having followed this way of working for four decades, a new manuscript arrived in my inbox at the same time as the final proofs for this booklet, in which the celebrity chefs included all preparation in the method. It suited that particular book but doesn't always work.

Quantity and description

Ingredients are given as the bought quantity and description, with the preparation following after a comma.

> 400g carrots, peeled and chopped
>
> 50g unsalted butter, diced

It is a common mistake to forget that the order in which the preparation is expressed can make a considerable difference to the quantity. Both the following examples are correct but which one is correct for that particular recipe depends on whether the author measured the pistachios before or after they were shelled. Proportions vary with the ingredient, of course, but you need twice as many pistachios in shell to give the same quantity as shelled pistachios.

>   100g pistachios, shelled

>   100g shelled pistachios

The same is true of all other nuts, fruits and vegetables that require peeling or other similar preparation.

>   apples, peeled, cored and chopped

>   dates, pitted

>   shelled walnuts

Use preparation terms consistently. For example, try to avoid using a mixture of 'thinly sliced' and 'finely sliced' in different recipes when they mean the same, as it may lead the reader to assume they are different. These are the most commonly used descriptions.

>   thinly sliced, thickly sliced, sliced 1cm thick

>   finely diced, diced, diced into bite-size pieces, diced into 1cm pieces

>   finely chopped, chopped, roughly chopped

If you adopt the above terms as the project style, you would maintain consistency by avoiding equivalent terms such as

>   finely sliced, roughly diced, chopped fine, coarsely chopped

Decide whether you need to include 'peeled' for vegetables, especially root vegetables. You do not usually include the extra instruction for items that you always treat in that way, such as onions. You would then specify if you leave on the skin (for a stock).

Even cans, jars and packets may need preparation. Cans may be drained or not; if you add an undrained can when it was supposed to be drained, you'll have too much liquid. Some ingredients need to be rinsed. The recipe may want you to reserve some of the syrup or liquid from a jar of fruit, add the fruit on its own or add it with the liquid.

> 400g can of red kidney beans, rinsed and drained
>
> 500g jar of stem ginger, drained and syrup reserved

Applying common sense

Use common sense when specifying ingredients, as getting it wrong can make nonsense of the text. This is particularly noticeable with herbs. For example, have you ever tried to measure fresh parsley or rosemary sprigs in a spoon? These simply don't make sense.

> ✘ 1 tbsp parsley
>
> ✘ 1 tbsp rosemary sprigs, chopped

Herbs are generally assumed to be fresh unless specified otherwise. Make the description suit what the recipe is actually using, whether that is just the leaves or the whole sprig. Remember that dried herbs are twice as pungent and not suitable for sprinkling or garnish. All the following options are correct. Choose your style and be clear and consistent.

> 1 sprig of rosemary, leaves picked and chopped
>
> 1 handful of parsley leaves, finely chopped
>
> 1 small bunch of parsley, roughly chopped
>
> 1 tbsp chopped rosemary
>
> 1 tsp chopped dried sage

7 | Preparation of ingredients

Complex preparation

The preparation instructions in the ingredients should contain everything the reader needs to know at a suitable level for their ability. If that amounts to more than two lines (at most), it should be moved into the method. For example, for a beginner or time-constrained readership, you might choose to use ready-prepared chestnuts rather than fresh and in the ingredients list they would be one of these simple options.

> 100g ready-prepared chestnuts, chopped
>
> 100g roasted and peeled chestnuts, chopped

If the recipe needed raw chestnuts, there are also options. For experienced readers, the following might be sufficient.

> 150g chestnuts, roasted, peeled and chopped

However, for a more general market, you would need to list the chestnuts, then set out more detailed preparation instructions at an appropriate point in the method.

> 150g whole chestnuts
>
> Preheat the oven to 200°C. Slit the skin of the chestnuts in a cross across the top using a sharp knife. Roast for 30 minutes. Leave until cool enough to handle, then peel off the skins and chop the nuts.

Don't repeat in the method any preparation already included in the ingredients list.

> ✘ 150g whole chestnuts, peeled and chopped
>
> ✘ Peel and chop the chestnuts.

8 | The method

The method should be a clear, chronological, step-by-step description of what is done with each ingredient, at what temperature, by what method and for how long, with a note of the end result of each process.

Ordering the text

As was noted at the beginning, think with your apron on.

Keep it sequential

In the method, you use each prepared ingredient in the order it appears in the ingredients list. If the preparation is included in the method (see **Complex preparation**), make sure it precedes using the item so the reader is not caught unawares, not having prepared something at the right time.

> Peel and roughly chop the mushrooms, then add them to the pan.
>
> ✘ Quickly add the mushrooms, which you have peeled and roughly chopped.

For a short recipe, you might use all the ingredients at once, so the method could be

> Put all the ingredients in a bowl and whisk thoroughly.

Sometimes you add several ingredients at once, but it is most usual to list them again in the method so the cook can easily check them off. It is better to avoid phrases such as 'add the next six ingredients'; it is not easy to count them or keep track and remember what the next six ingredients are. However, it is sometimes helpful to use 'add all the remaining ingredients' to keep things simple.

Paragraphs or numbers

Check the style preference for paragraphs or numbered/bulleted points. In either case, break the text where the method breaks; a pause should occur at the end of a process, not halfway through. The second example has been edited to make the breaks coincide with the practical pauses.

> ✘ 1. Bring the water to the boil in a large saucepan, add the beans. Cover and return to the boil. Simmer for 15 minutes, then drain the beans.

> 1. Bring the water to the boil in a large saucepan. Add the beans, cover and return to the boil. Simmer for 15 minutes.
> 2. Drain the beans.

Free-flowing text

Make sure the text is free-flowing but avoid sentences that are too long to follow easily. Definite articles and prepositions are generally used in the method to support the flow of text.

> Spread the potatoes in a layer over the top of the meat and garnish with a sprig of parsley.

> ✘ Spread potatoes in a layer over top of meat and garnish with sprig parsley.

Use the same or similar expressions consistently in each recipe for specific tasks rather than switching from one to another. Keeping this kind of subtlety in mind boosts the reader's trust and confidence in the text. For example, you might always use

> whisk the egg whites until they form soft peaks

rather than mixing it randomly with alternatives like

> beat the egg whites to soft-peak stage

> whisk the whites until soft peaks form

Abbreviations

While ingredients lists usually use contractions such as '1 tbsp', methods tend to use the full version, '1 tablespoon of'. Make sure this is done consistently.

> add 1 tablespoon of
>
> ✘ add 1 tbsp …

Numerals

While numerals are always used for quantities in the ingredients, both numerals and words are used in the method to ensure clarity. Use numerals for time and quantities, and words for equipment, proportion or repetition.

> Spoon 2 tablespoons of the coconut mixture into each of the two prepared pans, then spread each one with one-third of the chocolate mixture. Shake the pans gently three times to settle the mixture. Top each pan with half the remaining coconut mixture, then the remaining chocolate and 2 teaspoons of chopped nuts.

Equipment

If special equipment is essential for a recipe, it is usual to specify this in the introduction so the cook has prior warning. If there is an alternative method not using the specialist equipment, explain it in the method. For example, a description of making ice cream with an ice cream maker should be followed by a method for those who do not have one.

For most equipment, it will be enough to simply describe it in the method, giving a level of detail appropriate to the book. For saucepans and similar utensils, assume medium and specify small or large. For example, if the recipe starts with only a few ingredients then adds more later and therefore it is not obvious that the cook will need to start with a large saucepan, this should be indicated from the beginning.

> Heat the oil in a large saucepan, add the shallot and garlic and fry ... add 1 litre of the stock ...

The first mention in the method uses 'saucepan' in full; subsequently, just use 'pan'.

Suitable choices

Equipment must also be suitable for the cooking method, especially if that changes during the recipe. A casserole dish is assumed to be ovenproof, to use in the oven, but not flameproof, to use over direct heat. A saucepan is flameproof but not necessarily ovenproof.

> Heat the oil in a large ovenproof saucepan, add the shallot and garlic and fry ... transfer to the oven ...

Adequate descriptions

If the dimensions and detail of the equipment will materially affect the recipe, then you should be very specific. This is particularly important in baking. For example, the most common cake pan sizes are 18cm, 20cm and 23cm and are assumed to be round. You will get a different result if you bake the same cake mixture in a square or rectangular pan.

Each of these sizes is also available as a shallow or deep pan, a loose-bottomed pan or a springform pan (which has a loose base and a side that can be unclipped and removed separately). You need to specify if any of these types is used. A cheesecake made in a deep, fixed-base 20cm pan instead of a shallow springform 20cm pan would never leave the pan in one piece.

> Grease and line two 20cm cake pans
>
> Grease and line a 23cm shallow springform cake pan

When the recipe requires more than one of the same pan, be clear and consistent in the style you choose. Both of these are correct but not both in the same collection of recipes. You might want to mirror the style you have used for cans.

> two 20cm cake pans
>
> 2 × 20cm cake pans

Preparation in advance

If there is any advance preparation, such as overnight soaking, you may want to flag that up in the recipe introduction so no one starts the recipe without being able to complete it. In any event, such preparation should be the first point in the method.

> The beans need to be soaked overnight, then drained and rinsed before you start the recipe.

Oven temperatures

Include an instruction to preheat the oven so that the oven is at the cooking temperature when the dish goes in. For a roasted or baked dish, this is usually the first thing at the top of the method.

However, you need to allow only about ten minutes for the oven to heat to temperature, so if something else needs to be done first, move the preheating instruction to later in the method.

> Soak the beans in cold water for 20 minutes, then drain. Preheat the oven to 200°C/gas 8. Mix all the ingredients together ...
>
> ✘ Preheat the oven to 200°C/gas 8. Leave the dough to rise for about 1 hour until doubled in size, then bake ...

Use °C and gas, separating consistently either with an oblique or brackets. Very few publishers now use the term 'gas mark'. Add °F for international use.

> °C/gas or °C (gas)

The equivalent oven temperatures for °C and gas are standard and are given in the **conversion tables**. However, you will find that the equivalent temperatures are in the process of change so you need to be aware of how the author tested the recipes to make sure you use an appropriate set of temperature equivalents.

The most common oven temperature for baking most cakes has always compared a standard electric oven with a gas oven and this remains the convention in most published books.

> 180°C/gas 4

However, as electric ovens began to use fans, they vastly improved in reaching and maintaining oven temperatures, by as much as 20°C, so publishers began to specify the fan oven temperature.

> 180°C/160°C fan/gas 4

Almost all electric ovens are now fan ovens, so the most usual conversion used in new recipes is to specify just the fan oven temperature and the gas equivalent, without specifying 'fan oven'.

> 160°C/gas 4

There is always variability between the way different ovens behave, which is usually highlighted for inexperienced cooks in the **notes on the recipes**. It can also be useful to make mention there about fan ovens and temperatures.

Occasionally, you will find authors using a description of the oven temperature, such as a 'hot oven' (see **Oven temperature conversions**), but this is reserved for keeping things warm or other occasions when the specific temperature is not important.

> Put the meat in a warm oven while you finish the sauce.

Greasing and preparing equipment

Greasing, lining and otherwise preparing baking pans or equipment follows the preheating instructions.

> Grease and line two 20cm cake pans.

> Grease and line a 23cm shallow springform cake tin.

When the item is used, you would then refer to it as prepared.

> Spoon the mixture into the prepared pans.

Ingredient specifics

Only specify the detail of ingredients in the method if more than one type is listed in the ingredients. For example, there are two types of sugar listed in the following ingredients but only one type of flour, so the method needs to be specific for the sugar but can be general for the flour.

> 2 tbsp caster sugar
> 3 tbsp plain flour
> 2 tbsp dark soft brown sugar
>
> Add the caster sugar and flour and stir well, then stir in the brown sugar.

Here there is no need to be specific.

> 2 tbsp caster sugar
> 2 tbsp self-raising flour
> 1 tsp bicarbonate of soda
>
> Stir together the sugar, flour and bicarbonate of soda.

This extreme example would be confusing!

> ✘ 2 tbsp caster sugar
> ✘ 2 tbsp plain flour
> ✘ 1 tbsp self-raising flour
> ✘ 1 tsp dark soft brown sugar
>
> ✘ Mix the sugar and flour, then add the sugar.

Ingredients listed as optional are followed by ', if using' in the method. Alternative ingredients separated by 'or' are both listed in the method; a bracketed alternative is not listed in the method.

Techniques

How much detail will be required in the instructions will vary. If a technique is difficult to explain, you might suggest that an additional photograph or drawing could be useful to make it clear. If techniques occur frequently, you could include explanations in the supporting text and refer to them in the recipes.

How much explanation is needed?

A book for an experienced cook might describe whisking egg whites quite simply.

> Whisk the egg whites to soft peaks, then gradually fold in the icing sugar.

For a less experienced cook, it would be more helpful to give details.

> Put the egg whites in a large, grease-free bowl and use an electric or hand whisk to whisk them until they are fluffy and hold soft peaks when you lift the whisk from the mixture. Sift a little icing sugar over the top, then use a metal spoon to gently fold it in with a figure-of-eight motion, gradually adding the remaining icing sugar until it is all incorporated.

Most books would be somewhere in between.

Be aware of the subtleties of the method. Can you simply add the next ingredient or do you need to do it slowly? Do you stir all the time or not? Do you cover the pan or not? Is it important to use a metal spoon, as when folding icing sugar into egg whites? Have you adjusted the heat at particular points in the recipe? Sometimes giving a reason for a particular technique makes the whole process more meaningful.

> Using a metal spoon to keep as much air in the mixture as possible, gently fold the wet ingredients into the dry ingredients in a figure-of-eight motion until they are just mixed. The mixture may be a bit lumpy but if you overmix, your muffins will be tough.

Be aware of the practical difference between 'and' and 'then' because they clarify the sequence in which you do particular things, whether at the same time or one after the other. To emphasise this, the serial comma is rarely used before 'and' in cookery, but a comma is usually used before 'then'.

> Heat the oil in a pan until sizzling, then add the onions and garlic and stir well.

Timings and results

At each stage of the recipe, give timings and/or a description of what to expect and how the cook will know to move on to the next phase. This is called the 'doneness' test and is particularly important when the recipes are for inexperienced cooks.

> Simmer gently for about 2 minutes until thick and smooth.

> Bake the cake until well risen and beginning to shrink away from the side of the pan.

To emphasise that this is all part of one action point, there is no need for a comma before 'until'.

In some cases, there is likely to be more variation in the length of time different cooks take to complete a phase of the recipe. In such cases, it may be appropriate to use 'or until' instead of just 'until' and this should be preceded by a comma to indicate that the timing may vary. In the following example, cooking over a slightly higher heat may mean the sauce thickens sufficiently in three minutes instead of five, so the cook needs to concentrate on the results more than the clock.

> Mix over a gentle heat for about 5 minutes, or until the sauce coats the back of a spoon.

In any instructions, avoid telling the cook to act 'just before' something happens. An experienced cook may recognise the preceding stage but even that is not certain. It is much more helpful to describe the stage itself.

> Just as tiny bubbles form around the edge of the pan …
>
> ✘ Just before the sauce boils up the pan …

Subdividing the method

If you have **subdivided the ingredients**, then it is clearer for the reader if the method follows suit.

If an item in the ingredients list is a separate recipe, simply include it at the appropriate point in the recipe, using lower case. For example, if the ingredients list says

> 1 quantity White Sauce (see page xxx)

then the method will follow using lower case for the recipe name

> Stir in the white sauce

If the ingredients are divided by 'For the ...' subheadings, divide the method either with similar subheadings or with text starting the paragraphs with 'To make the ...'.

Using only part of an ingredient quantity

When the method doesn't use all of an ingredient at once, it should specify the amount to use or reserve, then say 'add the remaining [ingredient/reserved quantity]', as appropriate.

> 100g blueberries
>
> Reserve a few blueberries for decoration, then add the rest ...
>
> 100g chopped hazelnuts
>
> Add half the hazelnuts, mix well, then stir in the sugar. Add the remaining hazelnuts ...

9 | Recipes for international markets

Rather than creating several different editions, which used to be common practice, most publishers now design their cookery books to work for the whole English-speaking market. While this is perfectly logical from a cost, production and distribution point of view, it does raise some issues for the copyeditor to resolve and you may need to make some compromises.

This style of book is often referred to as 'mid-Atlantic' and this section focuses mainly on such books, which are primarily for the British market and use British English language styles, spellings and punctuation but include alternative measures and terminology for international markets, mainly the US and Australia.

Spellings and names

For international texts, ingredients, equipment and terminology use the British English terms and spellings. Where a word or phrase is completely different in other regions, the regional alternative is often put in brackets. In general, the alternative is not given if the difference is only one of spelling.

> courgettes (zucchini)
>
> chilli, travelling, flavour, mould, colour
>
> ✘ chilli (chili), travelling (traveling), flavour (flavor), mould (mold), colour (color)

9 | Recipes for international markets

If possible, avoid using any terms that highlight regional differences or words that have different meanings so could cause confusion, and instead choose words that work across all markets. As languages evolve, so will this list, so be aware of changing usage; for example, 'zucchini' is just beginning to be used in some recipes, and baking 'tin' is sometimes favoured over 'pan'.

> middle (not centre), baking parchment (not baking paper), kitchen foil (not tin foil or aluminium foil), baking pan (not tin)

A few publishers put the bracketed US English alternative in every case but it is more common to include them in the ingredients list rather than the method. Alternatives are not used in recipe titles so try to avoid British English words in titles, although this is not always possible.

Remember that some ingredients take a different alternative depending on form.

> coriander (cilantro) leaves
>
> coriander seeds
>
> ground coriander

Equipment or technique alternatives are only included on their first mention in the method. Remember that some words mean different things to cooks in different countries. British cooks 'grill' under a high, direct heat while US cooks 'broil'; US cooks 'grill' in a ridged griddle pan, which British cooks would describe as 'frying in a ridged griddle pan'.

Conversions

Almost all British authors work in metric and supply only the metric measures. Since cooks in America, Australia and some other countries use imperial, cup and spoon measurements, recipes marketed internationally will usually include all three options (or rarely just metric and imperial) and it will be your job to add them to the manuscript.

Publishers may include their preferred conversion tables in their house style. If not, you will need to draw up your own. To keep the ingredients lists as clear as possible, you will need to make choices and some compromises to maintain consistency while avoiding too many fractions.

There are plenty of tables available to use as a starting point or you may want to create your own by working out the exact equivalents and rounding them to practical quantities. In either case, scan through the book first before you start editing properly to establish that the conversions you have chosen work for the project.

Especially if an author uses very specific metric quantities, you may need to make some adjustments. For example, these are common conversions:

50g/1¾oz

60g/2oz

70g/2½oz

80g/2¾oz

But if the author frequently uses 55g or 75g, which is not unusual, you may want to adjust to 60g/2¼oz and 75g/2½oz and avoid using 70g.

9 | Recipes for international markets

You will already have established whether you are presenting the alternatives divided by obliques or brackets, or even listed in columns.

90ml/3fl oz/⅓ cup

90ml (3fl oz/⅓ cup)

Cooking with cups

If you are not familiar with cup measures, it is easy to buy a set of cup and spoon measures if you need them for reference. Cups obviously work by volume rather than weight, so they can be used for liquid or solid ingredients.

Some countries, such as Australia, specify a 250ml cup; others, including the US, favour a 240ml cup. If the decision has not been made by the client, decide which measure you are going to use and stick to it, although in practice it makes less difference than you might expect because a cup measure is inherently imprecise.

All cup measures are level, so you may need to use 'scant' and 'heaped' for solid ingredients or 'scant' and 'generous' for liquid ingredients to allow for this lack of subtlety. Sometimes, instead of using 'scant' and 'generous', a cup measure is listed with 'plus' or 'minus' teaspoons or tablespoons to give a more precise quantity.

120g (¾ cup minus 2 tbsp) caster (superfine) sugar

150g (1 cup plus 1 tbsp) self-raising (self-rising) flour

Liquid cup conversions are straightforward. For weights, it is more complicated because the same volume of denser ingredients – such as sugar – weighs more than the same volume of lighter ingredients – such as flaked almonds.

> 1 cup flaked almonds = about 80g
>
> 1 cup plain flour = about 125g
>
> 1 cup caster sugar = about 200g

The size of the ingredient and how it has been prepared also makes a difference to the quantity: beans or raspberries of different sizes, strawberries that have been thickly or thinly sliced, or finely or coarsely chopped almonds, for example.

This is made more complicated by the fact that US cooks usually prepare their ingredients before rather than after measuring, meaning that more of the ingredient fits in a cup; British practice is the reverse, so an equivalent cup measure is not always possible. It also contributes to the fact that you will find a baffling array of conversions, so decide on one that you trust and stick with it.

Some publishers classify ingredients into groups and use a simple conversion rate, like the ones provided in **Basic cup conversions**. In practical terms, this works well and is sufficiently accurate for most home cooking.

Other publishers have lengthy and complicated conversion rates that offer precise cup conversions for every type and subtype of ingredient. You should follow any such conversions provided by your client as they may not be the same for different publishers.

Temperatures and lengths

For international texts, oven temperatures need to be given in °F as well as °C and gas, while other temperatures (for sugar, for example) should also be in °C and °F.

Linear measurements need to be given in imperial as well as metric.

> 20cm/8in cake pan

Keeping it simple

Adding conversions can make ingredient listings long and rather ungainly. For example, the metric version of this recipe is simple and straightforward, but when you add the conversions, it can look off-putting.

> 90g/3¼oz/¾ cup plain (all-purpose) flour
>
> 1 egg
>
> 1 tsp bicarbonate of soda (baking soda)
>
> 75ml/2½fl oz/scant ⅓ cup vegetable oil
>
> 90g/3¼oz/scant ¼ cup dark soft brown sugar

If they are particularly complicated, you may want to discuss with the author whether '⅓ cup oil' and '¼ cup sugar' would be acceptable, which may be the case in some recipes.

Working from US English material

If you are working on a British edition of a US book, all this works in reverse, which throws up similar issues that demand different solutions.

If the book has been measured in imperial, in the earlier example of common conversions your original measure would be 2oz not 50g or 60g, which you would probably convert to 55g.

You also need to note that an imperial fluid ounce is smaller than a US fluid ounce, while an imperial pint is larger than a US pint.

Imperial fl oz = 28.4ml with 20fl oz to a pint = 568ml

US fl oz = 29.5ml with 16fl oz to a pint = 473ml

The difference in fl oz is so minimal that it makes little difference in practice. However, to avoid confusion, pints are not usually used in mid-Atlantic books as there is a greater margin for error.

As already noted, US recipes prepare ingredients before measuring, so if you are converting fully, you will need to calculate the original weight of the ingredients.

Layering for international books

When books were printed on four-colour plates, publishers began working together to produce books in several languages (including specifically US editions). All editions were printed from common colour plates, then overprinted with a text black plate specific to the language.

With the flexibility of digital printing and the facility for short runs, publishers still 'gang up' to make cost efficiencies, particularly in development, by publishing co-editions. This is now done with the language-specific text on one layer in the design program.

If you are working with layouts, you or the design team will need to make sure that all the text is on the correct layer. You may have to take into account that different languages take up more or less space than English by maintaining a very tight and specific word count on each section of the recipes.

It is the space taken by the language – not the word count alone – that is important, as this is affected by the length of words. French, Spanish and German, for example, will all take more space than English, even though German will have a lower word count.

10 | International conversions and alternatives

Some publishers will supply you with their own, more detailed house style and conversion sheets but these should provide basic information.

British (US) English cooking terms

aubergine (eggplant)	chilli (hot pepper) flakes
baking (cookie) sheet	Chinese leaves (stem lettuce)
baking parchment (not paper)	cling film (plastic wrap)
beetroot (beet)	cocoa (unsweetened chocolate) powder
bicarbonate of soda (baking soda)	coriander (cilantro) leaves (but note ground coriander)
biscuit (cookie)	cornflour (cornstarch)
black treacle (molasses)	cos (romaine) lettuce
broad (fava) beans	courgette (zucchini)
butter (lima) beans	crisps (potato chips)
casserole dish (Dutch oven)	crystallised (candied)
caster (superfine) sugar	dark chocolate with about 50% cocoa solids (semisweet)
celeriac (celery root)	dark chocolate with at least 70% cocoa solids (bittersweet)
chickpea (gram) flour	desiccated (dried shredded) coconut
chickpeas (garbanzos)	double (heavy) cream
chicory (endive)	eating (dessert) apple
chips (fries)	flaked (slivered) almonds

fry (sauté)	papaya (pawpaw)
frying pan (skillet)	paper towels (not kitchen paper)
golden (light corn) syrup	passata (sieved tomatoes)
grill (broil/broiler)	pitted (not stoned)
groundnut (peanut) oil	plain (all-purpose) flour
haricot (navy) bean	poussin (Cornish hen)
hazelnuts (filberts)	prawn (shrimp)
icing (frosting)	self-raising (self-rising) flour
icing (confectioners') sugar	single (light) cream
Kilner (Mason) jar	spring onion (scallion)
kitchen foil (not aluminium or tin)	sultanas (golden raisins)
mangetout (snow peas)	sweets (candy)
middle (not centre)	take-out (not takeaway)
muslin (cheesecloth)	tomato purée (paste)
pak choi (bok choi)	vanilla pod (bean)

Basic liquid conversions

Metric	Imperial	250ml cups
20ml	1½ tbsp	
50ml	3 tbsp	
60ml	2fl oz	¼ cup
75ml	2½fl oz	scant ⅓ cup
90ml	3fl oz	⅓ cup
100ml	3½fl oz	scant ½ cup
120ml	4fl oz	½ cup
150ml	5fl oz	scant ⅔ cup
175ml	6fl oz	¾ cup
200ml	7fl oz	scant 1 cup
225ml	8fl oz	scant 1 cup
250ml	8½fl oz	1 cup
300ml	10fl oz	1¼ cups
350ml	12¼fl oz	1½ cups
400ml	13fl oz	generous 1½ cups
450ml	15¾fl oz	scant 2 cups
500ml	17fl oz	2 cups
600ml	20fl oz	2½ cups
700ml	24fl oz	scant 3 cups
750ml	25fl oz	3 cups
800ml	28fl oz	3½ cups
900ml	32fl oz	3¾ cups
1 litre	34fl oz	4 cups
1.5 litres	56fl oz	6⅔ cups

Basic weight conversions

Metric	Imperial
50g	2oz
75g	2½oz
100g	3½oz
125g	4oz
150g	5oz
175g	6oz
200g	7oz
225g	8oz
250g	9oz
300g	10½oz
350g	12oz
400g	14oz
450g	1lb

Basic cup conversions

This is a very simple table and many publishers will supply more detailed conversions. You could also look at *Measurements for Cooking* by Delora Jones, which gives a huge amount of detail on US cooking.

Grams per cup	Food type	¾ cup	½ cup	¼ cup
300g	preserves and syrups condensed milk peanut butter	225g	150g	75g
250g	red lentils small pulses yogurt	185g	125g	60g
200g	rice dried beans green lentils caster sugar	150g	100g	50g
150g	seeds raisins pitted olives couscous cocoa powder	110g	75g	35g
125g	flour whole nuts	90g	60g	30g
100g	fine dry breadcrumbs ground nuts	75g	50g	25g
80g	flaked almonds	60g	40g	20g
50g	finely chopped herb leaves, such as parsley	40g	25g	15g

10 | International conversions and alternatives

Oven temperature conversions

°C (fan)	°F (fan equivalent)	°C (non-fan)	Gas	Description
90°C	190°F	110°C	gas ¼	Very cool
100°C	210°F	120°C	gas ½	
120°C	250°F	140°C	gas 1	Cool
130°C	265°F	150°C	gas 2	
140°C	280°F	160°C	gas 3	Moderate
160°C	320°F	180°C	gas 4	
170°C	340°F	190°C	gas 5	Moderately hot
180°C	350°F	200°C	gas 6	
190°C	375°F	220°C	gas 7	Hot
200°C	400°F	230°C	gas 8	
220°C	425°F	240°C	gas 9	Very hot

Linear measurement conversions and pan sizes

mm/cm	Inches
2–3mm	⅛in
5mm	¼in
1cm	½in
2.5cm	1in
4cm	1½in
6cm	2½in
10cm	4in
15cm	6in
18cm	7in
20cm	8in
23cm	9in
25cm	10in
30cm	12in

11 | Additional notes

There are a few other things to remember when preparing a cookery typescript for layout. Check with your client whether these issues are relevant and include them on your style sheet.

Fonts and symbols

Some special characters do not convert automatically so check with the client how to supply anything but the most common symbols.

These special sorts are usually acceptable:

- common fractions: ¼, ½, ¾
- basic symbols: ©, @, %, °
- simple accented letters, such as purée, café, sauté, à la carte, crêpe, *grünen Salate*.

When you do use symbols, use the correct one, not a superscript 'o' for a degree sign, for example.

Any more unusual symbols do not transfer and should be unformatted, as listed below for fractions, surrounded by square brackets or highlighted. This avoids any potential for confusion in numbers with fractions:

- any other fractions, such as 1/3, 2/3, 1/8, 5/8
- diacritics, such as Polish or Scandinavian accents
- unusual symbols, such as ™, ç, š, ~, ø.

11 | Additional notes

Automating tasks on cookery manuscripts

On any text, it is worth considering the value of automating some of the simpler editorial tasks to speed up the editing process, ensure you don't miss anything, and allow you to concentrate on the more complicated elements.

Whether you are using a simple Find and Replace, an AutoText, a macro or a commercial editing program, you should be aware of some pitfalls particularly relevant to cookery that you should watch out for when setting up automated tasks:

- Step through changes one at a time using Replace rather than Replace All so you avoid getting replacements or alternatives where you don't want them. For example, US English alternatives for ingredient names are not generally included in titles.
- Also take care with plurals, as searching for 'aubergine' and replacing it with 'aubergine (eggplant)' could give you '2 aubergine (eggplant)s'.
- Unintended changes can also sneak into other unexpected places. Replacing 'pan' with 'saucepan' could give you 'cake saucepan', 'accomsaucepany', 'exsaucepand' and 'saucepantry'. Adding 'unsalted' to all the instances of 'butter' will give you 'unsalted butter the pan'.
- Being specific on spacing around your changes is crucial, especially around measurements.
- Always specify Match Case to refine your search to the specific item you are searching for.
- Avoid AutoText instructions that you are likely to type in normal text. Setting up 'ufgb' for 'until firm and golden brown' could be useful in a baking book and is not something you would otherwise type. However, being offered 'peel and slice the apples' whenever you type 'pasta' is not so helpful.

12 | Proofreading recipes

As I indicated at the start, when re-reading text you have written, or which you have already read many times, the brain automatically begins to generalise what you see, reading what you expect to be there rather than what is actually there. This is why recipe text should be proofread by a professional. It is not a good idea for an author alone to proofread their own recipes, or even for the copyeditor to do the proofread.

There are particular things in cookery texts that the proofreader should look out for:

- Check that the copyeditor has applied the conversions and international notation according to the style sheet, keeping in mind that some common-sense adjustments may have been made.
- In print books and texts, be especially aware of widows and orphans, which can occur more often in text set over a narrow column width.
- Make sure the spacing between quantity and measure is to style.
- Check there are no spaces between a number and a following fraction.
- Resolve any line breaks that separate a quantity from a measure.
- Ideally, a recipe should be displayed on a single spread, to avoid having to turn a page while you are trying to stir ingredients or while your hands are sticky.
- Look out for short, cramped or badly spaced lines, again especially on narrow column widths.
- Be aware of any last-minute changes that were made to recipes – chicken for fish, for example, in which not every implication of the change has been picked up, such as using chicken stock.
- Check that no conversions have been omitted.

13 | Applying cookery editing skills to other texts

This guide has been written for copyeditors of cookery books and recipe texts, so the examples and specifics are food-related. However, with the application of a little imagination, it is not difficult to see that similar principles apply to working on all step-by-step texts, such as DIY, craft or art projects. Even organisational books – lifestyle organisers, wedding planners – can benefit from a similar approach.

The common factor is that you are ensuring that the practical application of a set of skills has the finished result the author intends. Constantly put yourself in the position of the reader and remind yourself of the physical activity they are performing. With appropriate substitutes for 'ingredient', 'temperature' and so on, that is exactly what you have been learning throughout this guide.

In any instructional text, make sure the content tells the reader everything they need to know to successfully complete the project. Here is a checklist to get you started:

- Define the audience so you can include the required level of detail.
- Establish a rapport and level of trust that the text won't let the reader down.
- Make the projects worth the effort.
- Think 'hands-on'; the reader is working in three dimensions.
- Explain terminology and background up front.
- Instruct the reader to gather the materials they need before they start.
- Address any safety issues.
- Make it clear how to proceed in the right sequence.
- Organise the information so it is easy for the reader to find what they are looking for.

- Don't leave the reader guessing.
- Remember the reader shouldn't be left with the proverbial one screw when they have put everything together.
- Make sure the presentation is consistent.
- Ensure the finished result is achievable.

Hopefully this guide will have given you the basics of good practice in copyediting recipe texts and you can use that knowledge to expand your skills across other practical subjects.

About the author

In publishing since 1975, Wendy Hobson has worked both in-house as a commissioning editor and editorial director and for many years as a freelance writer and editor. The focus of her work has been primarily on trade books on a range of lifestyle issues, heavily featuring cookery, practical crafts and life organisation. She has also tested many cookery books, and written several cookery books, lifestyle guides and organisers. She has been commissioned by a range of cookery publishers for both editing and writing, including Nourish, Hardie Grant, Welbeck, BBC Books, Foulsham and Arcturus. Adept at nurturing new authors, such as Nisha Katona, she has also worked with seasoned professionals like Nicola Graimes and Carolyn Humphries, and not a few celebrities, including Madhur Jaffrey, Ken Hom, Gary Rhodes and Mary Berry.

Acknowledgements

I think of publishing as a team activity, so to everyone involved in the countless cookery books I have had the pleasure (usually a pleasure!) to work on over the years, thank you so much for the challenges, the successes and the opportunities to learn – and to keep on learning – about so many aspects of food, cooking and publishing. This guide is the result of that experience and I hope it shares knowledge that editors new to this field will find useful.

It has benefited enormously from the input of my CIEP colleagues Liz Jones, Cathy Tingle, Margaret Hunter, Myriam Birch and Michelle Bullock, and their ideas and suggestions. Thanks, too, to the beta readers, Anna Williams and Kate Berens, for their constructive comments.

Bon appetit!

www.ingramcontent.com/pod-product-compliance
Lightning Source LLC
Chambersburg PA
CBHW071759080526
44588CB00013B/2310